The Nursery Rhyme Book

Amsco Music Publishing Company

Distributed by Music Sales Limited
14-15 Berners Street, London W1T 3LJ, UK.

The Nursery Rhyme Book
UK   AM 26824
UK   ISBN 0 86001 815 6
USA   770012-3
USA   ISBN 0 8256 9337 3

The Rhymes

The Songs

4

Baa, Baa, Black Sheep

Baa, baa, black sheep, have you an-y wool? Yes, sir, yes, sir,

three bags full; One for the mas - ter, and one for the

dame, and one for the lit - tle boy that lives down the lane.

Girls and Boys Come Out to Play

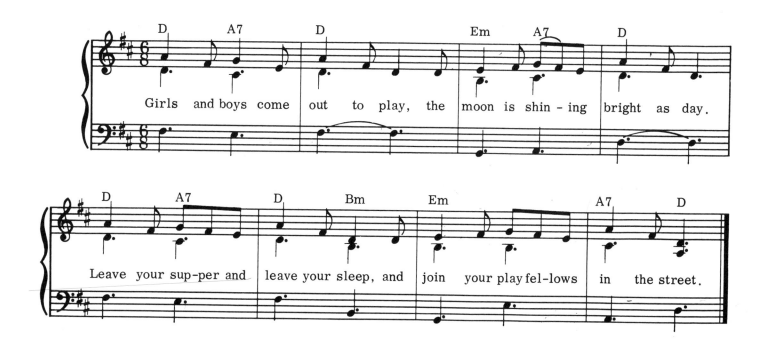

Girls and boys come out to play, the moon is shin-ing bright as day.

Leave your sup-per and leave your sleep, and join your play fel-lows in the street.

HERE ARE THE LADY'S KNIVES AND FORKS

Here are the lady's knives and forks,
Here is the lady's table,
Here is the lady's looking-glass,
And here is the baby's cradle.

HERE IS THE CHURCH, AND HERE IS THE STEEPLE

Here is the church, and here is the steeple;
Open the door and here are the people.
Here is the parson going upstairs,
And here he is a-saying his prayers.

HARK, HARK, THE DOGS DO BARK

Hárk, hark, the dogs do bark,
The beggars are coming to town;
Some in rags, and some in jags,
And one in a velvet gown.

CROSS-PATCH

Cross-patch, draw the latch,
Sit by the fire and spin;
Take a cup, and drink it up,
Then call your neighbours in.

Bobby Shaftoe

Bob-by Shaf-toe's | gone to sea,— | sil-ver buck-les | on his knee;— | He'll come back and | mar-ry me,— | Bon-ny Bob-by | Shaf-toe. | Bob-by Shaf-toe's | bright and fair, | comb-ing down his | yel-low hair; | He's my ain for- | ev-er-mair, | Bon-ny Bob-by | Shaf-toe.

I HAD A LITTLE PONY

I had a little pony,
His name was Dapple Gray;
I lent him to a lady
To ride a mile away.
She whipped him, she slashed him,
She rode him through the mire;
I would not lend my pony now,
For all the lady's hire.

BOW-WOW, SAYS THE DOG

Bow-wow, says the dog,
Mew, mew, says the cat,
Grunt, grunt, goes the hog,
And squeak goes the rat.
Tu-whu, says the owl,
Caw, caw, says the crow,
Quack, quack, says the duck,
And what the cuckoos say you know.

The Barnyard Song

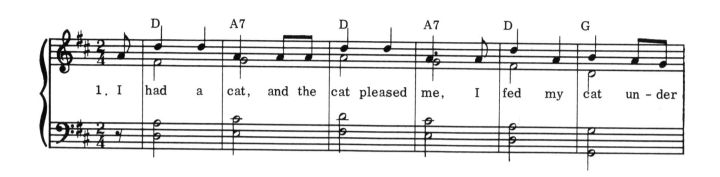

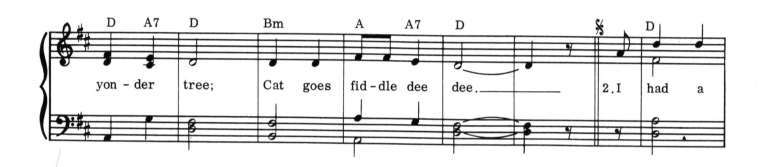

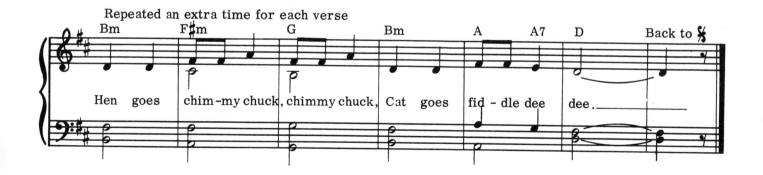

Ding Dong Bell

IF WISHES WERE HORSES

If wishes were horses
Beggars would ride;
If turnips were watches
I would wear one by my side.

IF I HAD A DONKEY

If I had a donkey that wouldn't go,
Would I beat him? Oh no, no.
I'd put him in the barn and give him some corn,
The best little donkey that ever was born.

BYE, BABY BUNTING

Bye, baby bunting,
Daddy's gone a-hunting,
Gone to get a rabbit skin
To wrap the baby bunting in.

COCK A DOODLE DOO

Cock a doodle doo!
My dame has lost her shoe,
My master's lost his fiddling stick,
And knows not what to do.

Turn Again, Whittington

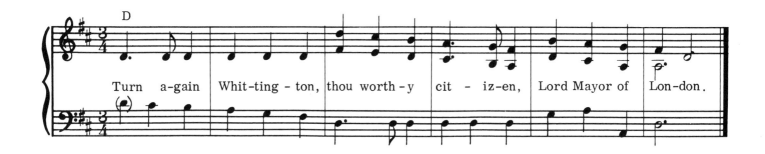

Turn a-gain Whit-ting-ton, thou worth-y cit-iz-en, Lord Mayor of Lon-don.

Doctor Foster

Doc-tor Fos-ter went to Glouces-ter in a show-er of rain, he stepped in a pud-dle, right up to his mid-dle, and nev-er went there a-gain.

The Farmer in the Dell

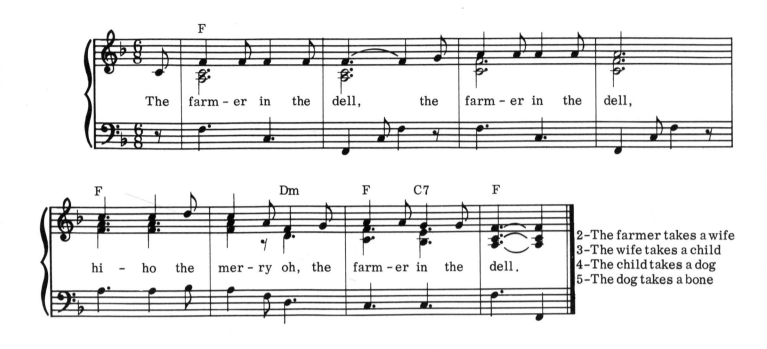

The farm - er in the dell, the farm - er in the dell,

hi - ho the mer - ry oh, the farm - er in the dell.

2-The farmer takes a wife
3-The wife takes a child
4-The child takes a dog
5-The dog takes a bone

Frère Jacques

Frè - re Jac-ques, Frè - re Jac-ques, Dor-mez vous? Dor-mez vous?
Are you sleep-ing? Are you sleep-ing? Broth-er John, Broth-er John.

Son-nez les ma - ti - nes, son-nez les ma - ti - nes, din don din! Din don din!
Morn-ing bells are ring - ing, morn-ing bells are ring - ing, ding ding dong! Ding ding dong!

The Grand Old Duke of York

I SAW A SHIP A-SAILING

I saw a ship a-sailing,
A-sailing on the sea,
And oh, but it was laden
With pretty things for thee!

Goosey, Goosey Gander

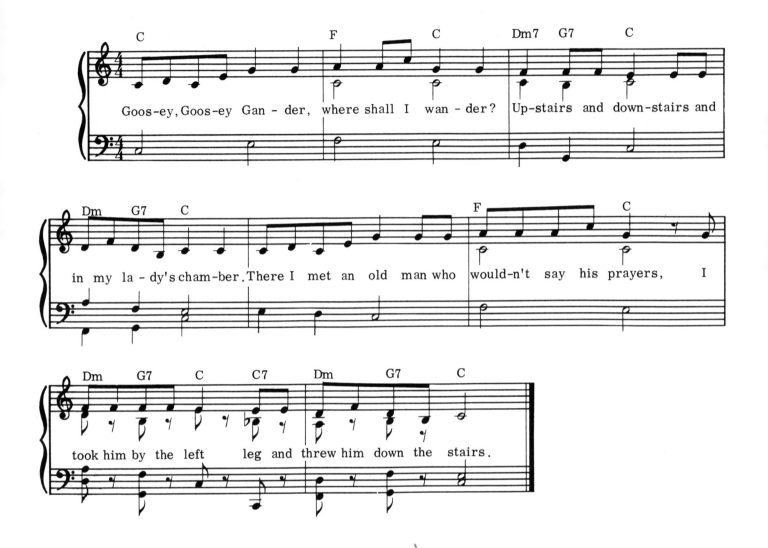

Goos-ey, Goos-ey Gan - der, where shall I wan - der? Up-stairs and down-stairs and in my la - dy's cham-ber. There I met an old man who would-n't say his prayers, I took him by the left leg and threw him down the stairs.

LITTLE POLLY FLINDERS

Little Polly Flinders sat among the cinders,
Warming her pretty little toes;
Her mother came and caught her,
And whipped her little daughter
For spoiling her nice new clothes.

LITTLE TOMMY TUCKER

Little Tommy Tucker sings for his supper:
What shall we give him? White bread and butter.
How shall he cut it without e'er a knife?
How will he be married without e'er a wife?

Georgie Porgie

Geor- gie Por - gie, pud-ding and pie, kissed the girls and made them cry.

When the boys came out to play, Geor - gie Por - gie ran a - way.

CURLY LOCKS, CURLY LOCKS

Curly locks, curly locks,
Wilt thou be mine?
Thou shalt not wash dishes
Nor yet feed the swine;
But sit on a cushion
And sew a fine seam,
And feed upon strawberries,
Sugar and cream.

14

Hey Diddle Diddle

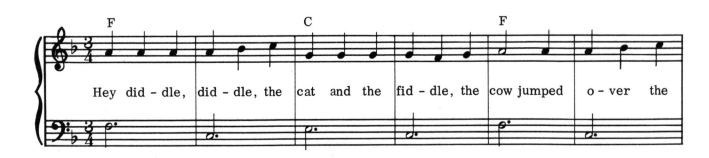

Hey did - dle, did - dle, the cat and the fid - dle, the cow jumped o - ver the

moon. _____ The lit - tle dog laughed _____ to see such fun, and the dish ran a-

way with the spoon. _____

Hickory, Dickory Dock

Hick-or- y, dick-or- y dock, the mouse ran up the clock. The
clock struck one, the mouse ran down, hick-or- y dick-or- y dock.

Handy Spandy

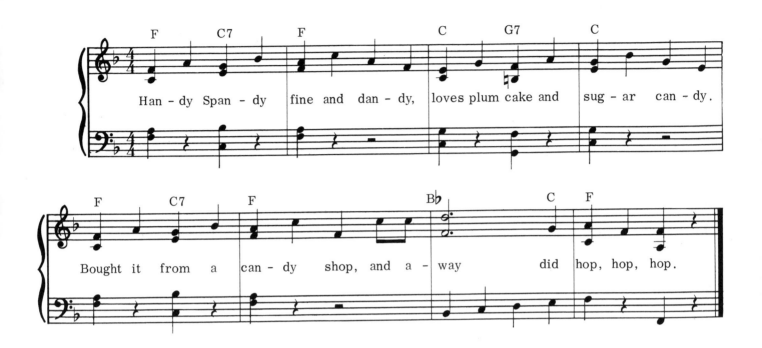

Hush, Little Baby

Humpty Dumpty

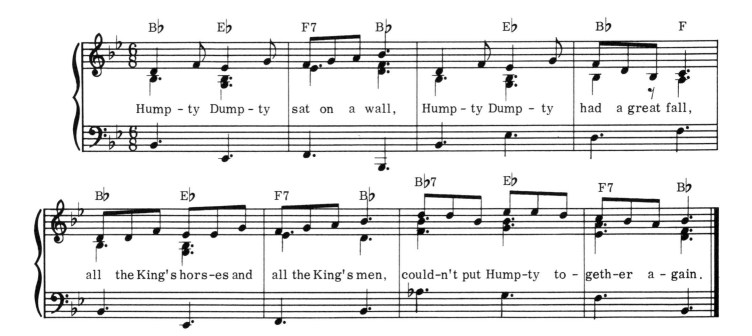

18

Here We Go Gathering Nuts in May

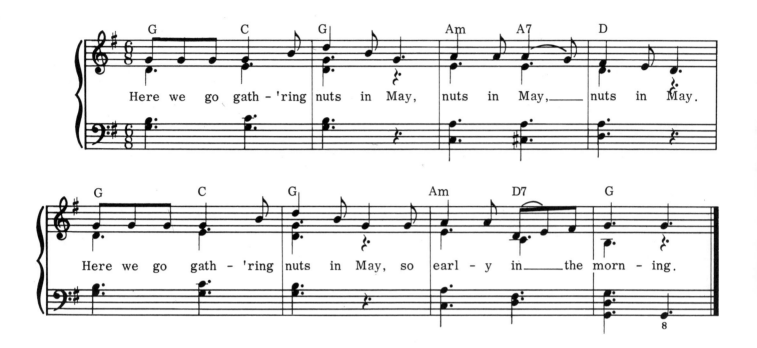

PRETTY MAID

Pretty maid, pretty maid,
Where have you been?
Gathering roses
To give to the Queen.
Pretty maid, pretty maid,
What gave she you?
She gave me a diamond,
As big as my shoe.

ROSES ARE RED

Roses are red,
Violets are blue,
Sugar is sweet
And so are you.

ONE, TWO, THREE

One, two, three, I love coffee,
And Billy loves tea,
How good you be,
One, two, three, I love coffee,
And Billy loves tea.

ONE, TWO, THREE, FOUR

One, two, three, four,
Mary at the cottage door,
Five, six, seven, eight,
Eating cherries off a plate.

I Love Little Pussy

I___ love lit - tle pus - sy, her coat is so warm, and___ if I don't hurt her she'll

do me no___ harm.

RIDE A COCK-HORSE

Ride a cock-horse to Banbury Cross,
To see a fine lady upon a white horse;
Rings on her fingers and bells on her toes,
And she shall have music wherever she goes.

RUB-A-DUB-DUB

Rub-a-dub-dub, three men in a tub,
And how do you think they got there?
The butcher, the baker, the candlestick-maker,
They all jumped out of a rotten potato,
'Twas enough to make a man stare.

ONE, TWO, THREE, FOUR, FIVE

One, two, three, four, five,
Once I caught a fish alive,
Six, seven, eight, nine, ten,
Then I let it go again.
Why did you let it go?
Because it bit my finger so.
Which finger did it bite?
The little finger on the right

Here We Go Round the Mulberry Bush

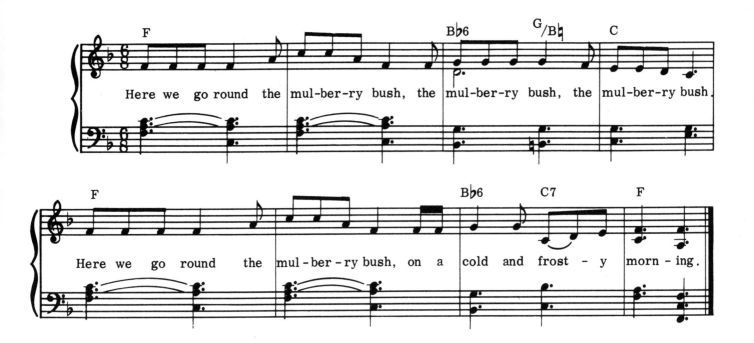

Here we go round the mul-ber-ry bush, the mul-ber-ry bush, the mul-ber-ry bush.

Here we go round the mul-ber-ry bush, on a cold and frost-y morn-ing.

THERE WAS AN OLD WOMAN WHO LIVED IN A SHOE

There was an old woman who lived in a shoe,
She had so many children she didn't know what to do;
She gave them some broth without any bread;
She whipped them all soundly and put them to bed.

DIDDLETY, DIDDLETY, DUMPTY

Diddlety, diddlety, dumpty,
The cat ran up the plum tree;
Half a crown to fetch her down,
Diddlety, diddlety, dumpty.

Jack and Jill

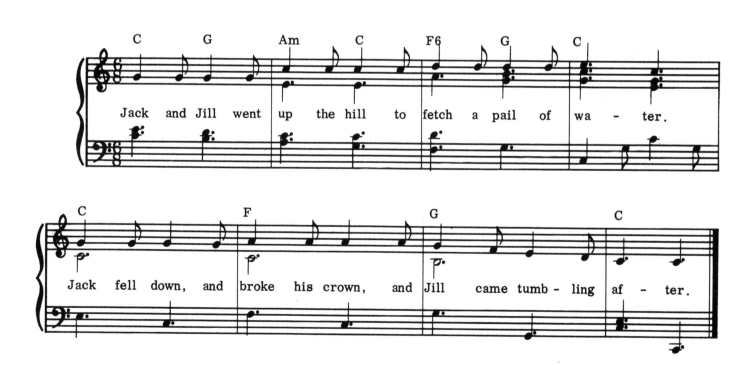

Little Bo-peep

Lit-tle Bo-peep has lost her sheep, and does-n't know where to find them.

Leave them a-lone, and they'll come home, bring-ing their tails be-hind them.

Little Boy Blue

Lit-tle Boy Blue, come blow your horn, the sheep's in the mead-ow, the cow's in the corn.

Where's the boy who looks af-ter the sheep? He's un-der the hay-stack fast a-sleep.

Will you wak-en him? No, not I, for if I do,—he's sure to cry.

London Bridge is Falling Down

Lon - don Bridge is fall - ing down, fall - ing down, fall - ing down, Lon - don Bridge is

fall - ing down, my fair la - dy.

PETER, PETER, PUMPKIN EATER

Peter, Peter, pumpkin eater,
Had a wife and couldn't keep her;
He put her in a pumpkin shell
And there he kept her very well.

LITTLE FISHES IN A BROOK

Little fishes in a brook,
Father caught them on a hook,
Mother fried them in a pan,
Johnnie eats them like a man.

Ladybird, Ladybird

Lad-y-bird, lad-y-bird, fly a-way home, your house is on fire and your child-ren all gone.

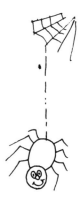

Little Miss Muffet

Lit-tle Miss Muf-fet sat on a tuf-fet eat-ing her curds and whey._____ There came a big spi-der who sat down be-side her and fright-ened Miss Muf-fet a - way._____

Little Jack Horner

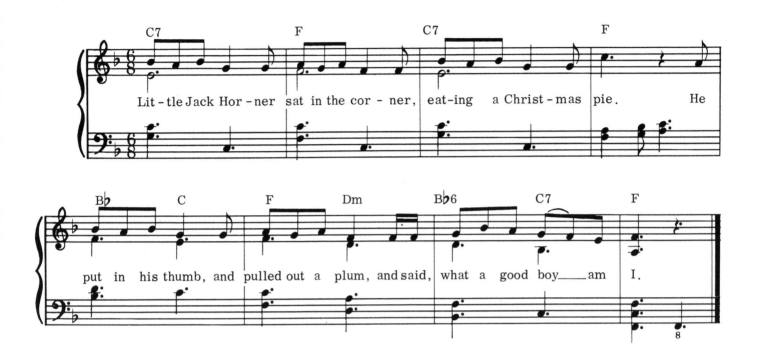

Lit-tle Jack Hor-ner sat in the cor-ner, eat-ing a Christ-mas pie. He put in his thumb, and pulled out a plum, and said, what a good boy___am I.

Mary Had a Little Lamb

Ma-ry had a lit-tle lamb, lit-tle lamb, lit-tle lamb, Ma-ry had a lit-tle lamb, its fleece was white as snow.

The Muffin Man

I'M THE KING OF THE CASTLE

I'm the king of the castle,
Get down you dirty rascal.

Mary, Mary, Quite Contrary

Diddle, Diddle Dumpling, My Son John

Old MacDonald

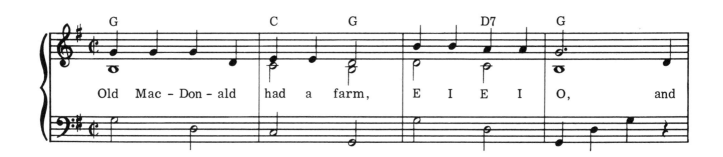

Old Mac-Don-ald had a farm, E I E I O, and

on that farm he had some sheep,* E I E I O. With a

**baa baa here, baa baa there, here a baa, there a baa, ev-'ry-where a baa baa.

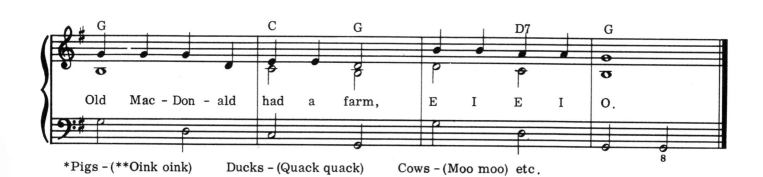

Old Mac-Don-ald had a farm, E I E I O.

*Pigs - (**Oink oink) Ducks - (Quack quack) Cows - (Moo moo) etc.

Oranges and Lemons

Old Mother Hubbard

Verse 1

Old Moth-er Hub-bard, she went to the cup-board, to fetch her poor dog a bone.

When she got there the cup-board was bare, and so the poor dog had none.

Verses 2 - 14

She went to the baker's to buy him some bread, but when she came back the poor dog was dead.

Extra Verses

She went to the undertaker's
To buy him a coffin;
But when she came back
The poor dog was laughing.

She took a clean dish
To get him some tripe;
But when she came back
He was smoking a pipe.

She went to the fishmonger's
To buy him some fish;
But when she came back
He was licking the dish.

She went to the tavern
For white wine and red;
But when she came back
The dog stood on his head.

She went to the fruiterer's
To buy him some fruit;
But when she came back
He was playing the flute.

She went to the tailor's
To buy him a coat;
But when she came back
He was riding a goat.

She went to the hatter's
To buy him a hat;
But when she came back
He was feeding the cat.

She went to the barber's
To buy him a wig;
But when she came back
He was dancing a jig.

She went to the cobbler's
To buy him some shoes;
But when she came back
He was reading the news.

She went to the seamstress
To buy him some linen;
But when she came back
The dog was a-spinning.

She went to the hosier's
To buy him some hose;
But when she came back
He was dressed in his clothes.

The dame made a curtsey,
The dog made a bow;
The dame said, Your servant,
The dog said, Bow-wow.

Pat-a-cake, Pat-a-cake, Baker's Man

Pat - a - cake, pat - a - cake, ba-ker's man, bake me a cake as

fast as you can. Pat it and prick it, and mark it with 'B',

put it in the ov - en for Ba - by and me.

TWO LITTLE DICKY BIRDS

Two little dicky birds, sitting on a wall;
One named Peter, the other named Paul.
Fly away Peter! Fly away Paul!
Come back, Peter! Come back, Paul!

Oh Dear! What Can the Matter Be?

Oh Dear! What can the mat-ter be? Dear dear! What can the mat-ter be?

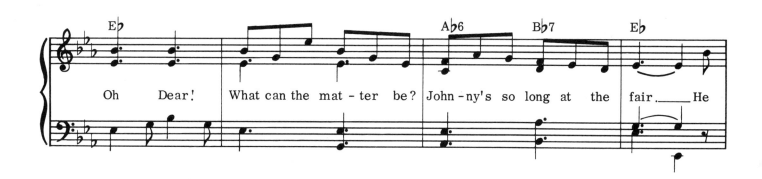

Oh Dear! What can the mat-ter be? John-ny's so long at the fair. ____ He

promised to buy me a bunch of blue rib-bons, he promised to buy me a bunch of blue rib-bons, he

prom-ised to buy me a bunch of blue rib-bons, to tie up my bon-nie brown hair.

Old King Cole

Pease Porridge Hot

Pease por-ridge hot, pease por-ridge cold, pease por-ridge in the pot

nine days old.

Pop Goes the Weasel

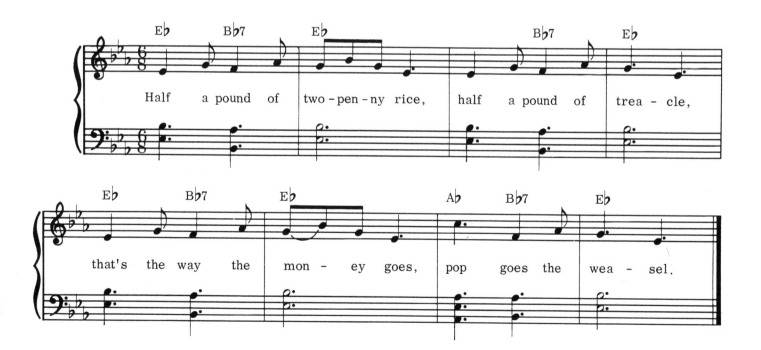

Half a pound of two-pen-ny rice, half a pound of trea-cle,

that's the way the mon-ey goes, pop goes the wea-sel.

Pussy Cat, Pussy Cat

Pus-sy cat, pus-sy cat, where have you been? I've been—to Lon-don to vis- it the Queen.

Pus-sy cat, pus-sy cat, what did you there? I frightened a lit-tle mouse un-der her chair.

JACK BE NIMBLE

Jack be nimble,
Jack be quick,
Jack jump over
The candlestick.

Polly Put the Kettle On

THERE WAS A LITTLE GIRL

There was a little girl, and she had a little curl
Right in the middle of her forehead;
When she was good she was very, very good,
But when she was bad she was horrid.

THERE WAS A LITTLE MAN

There was a little man, and he had a little gun,
And his bullets were made of lead, lead, lead;
He went to the brook, and shot a little duck,
Right through the middle of the head, head, head.

Rock-a-bye Baby

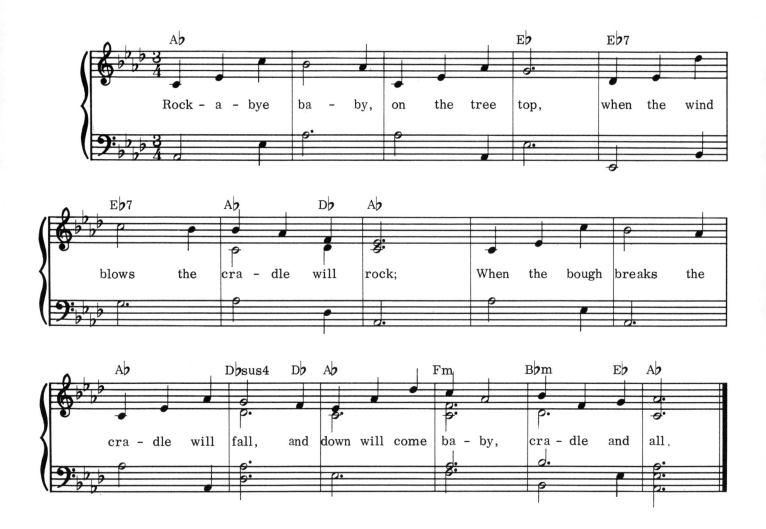

IT'S RAINING, IT'S POURING

It's raining, it's pouring,
The old man's snoring;
He got into bed and bumped his head
And couldn't get up in the morning.

RAIN, RAIN, GO AWAY

Rain, rain, go away,
Come again another day,
Little Johnny wants to play.

Ring-a-Ring o' Roses

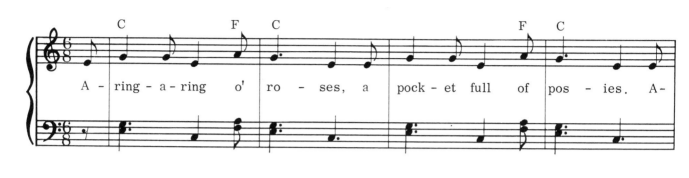

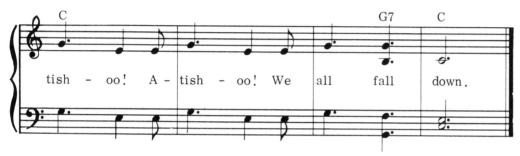

Row, Row, Row Your Boat

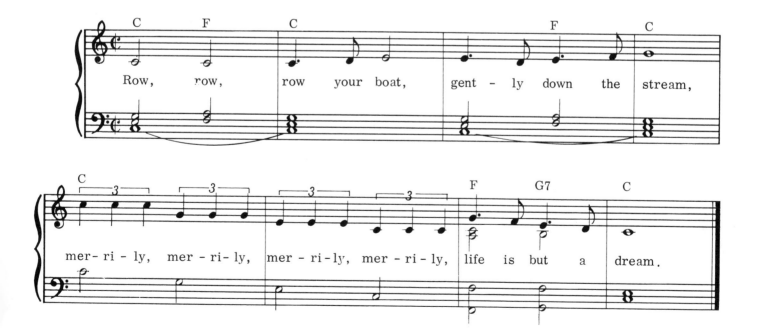

See-Saw, Margery Daw

Simple Simon

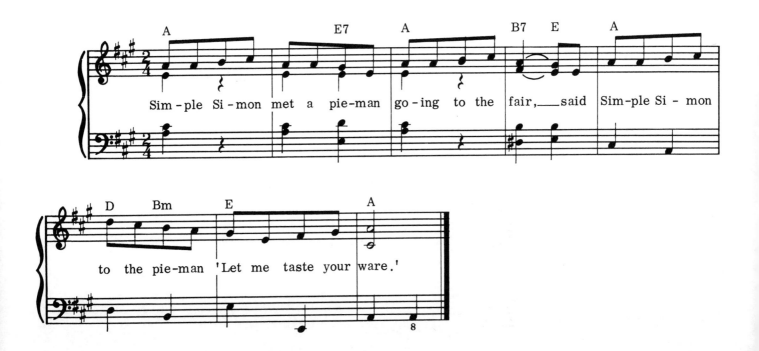

Sing a Song of Sixpence

Ten Little Indians

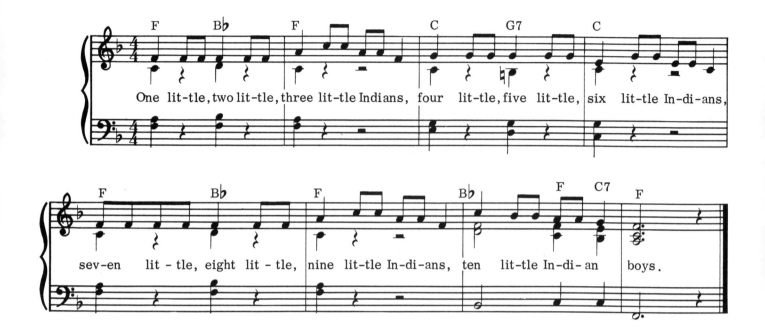

seven little, eight little, nine little Indians, ten little Indian boys.

SOLOMON GRUNDY

Solomon Grundy,
Born on a Monday,
Christened on Tuesday,
Married on Wednesday;
Took ill on Thursday,
Worse on Friday,
Died on Saturday,
Buried on Sunday.
This is the end
Of Solomon Grundy.

There Was a Crooked Man

HICKETY, PICKETY, MY BLACK HEN

Hickety, pickety, my black hen,
She lays eggs for gentlemen;
Gentlemen come every day
To see what my black hen doth lay.

This Little Pig Went to Market

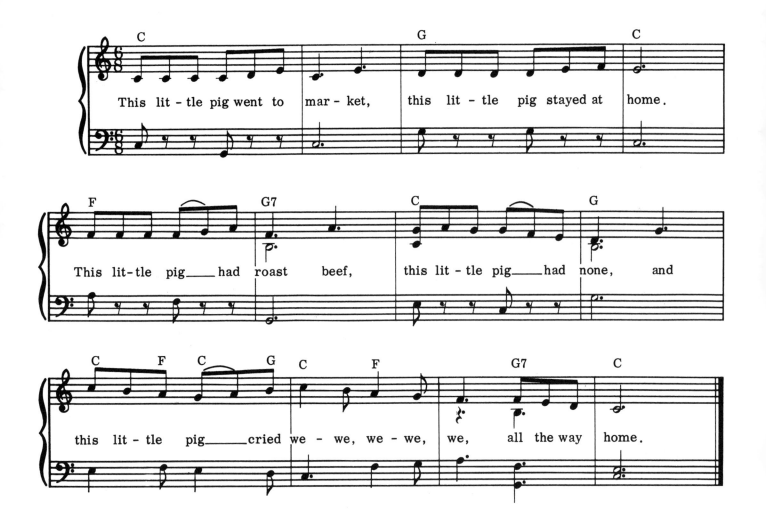

TO MARKET, TO MARKET

To market, to market,
To buy a fat pig,
Home again, home again,
Jiggety-jig.
To market, to market,
To buy a fat hog,
Home again, home again,
Jiggety-jog.

Twinkle, Twinkle Little Star

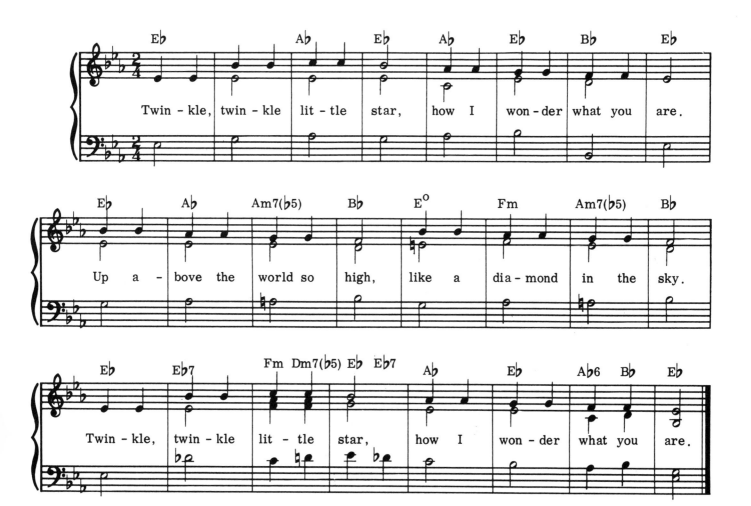

46

Three Blind Mice

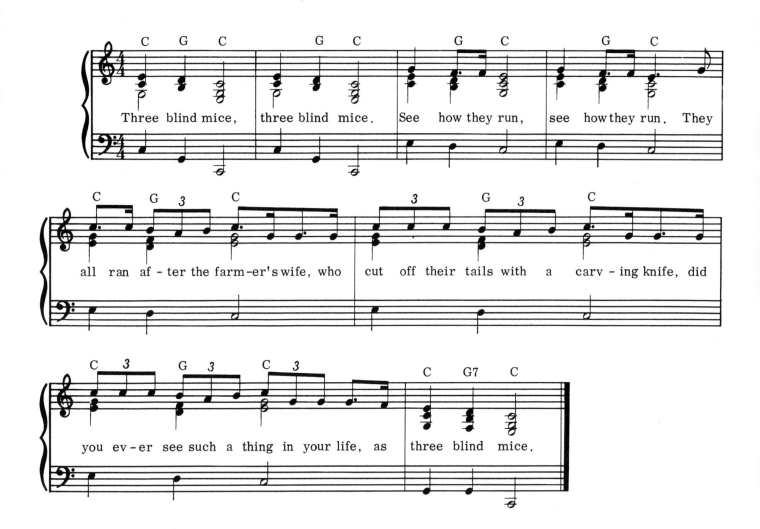

Three blind mice, three blind mice. See how they run, see how they run. They all ran af-ter the farm-er's wife, who cut off their tails with a carv-ing knife, did you ev-er see such a thing in your life, as three blind mice.

Tom, Tom the Piper's Son

Tom, Tom, the pip-er's son, stole a pig and a-way he run; The pig was eat, and

Tom was beat, and Tom went howl-ing down the street.

OLD MOTHER GOOSE

Old Mother Goose,
When she wanted to wander,
Would ride through the air
On a very fine gander.

Mother Goose had a house,
'Twas built in a wood,
Where an owl at the door
For sentinel stood.

She had a son Jack,
A plain-looking lad,
He was not very good,
Nor yet very bad.

She sent him to market,
A live goose he bought;
See, mother, says he,
I have not been for nought.

Jack's goose and her gander
Grew very fond;
They'd both eat together,
Or swim in the pond.

Jack found one fine morning,
As I have been told,
His goose had laid him
An egg of pure gold.

Jack ran to his mother
The news for to tell,
She called him a good boy,
And said it was well.

Jack sold his golden egg
To a merchant untrue,
Who cheated him out of
A half of his due.

Then Jack went a-courting
A lady so gay,
As fair as the lily,
And sweet as the May.

The merchant and squire
Soon came at his back,
And began to belabour
The sides of poor Jack.

Then old Mother Goose
That instant came in,
And turned her son Jack
Into famed Harlequin.

She then with her wand
Touched the lady so fine,
And turned her at once
Into sweet Columbine.

The gold egg in the sea
Was thrown away then,
When an odd fish brought her
The egg back again.

The merchant then vowed
The goose he would kill,
Resolving at once
His pockets to fill.

Jack's mother came in,
And caught the goose soon,
And mounting its back,
Flew up to the moon.

Oh, Where, Oh, Where Has My Little Dog Gone?

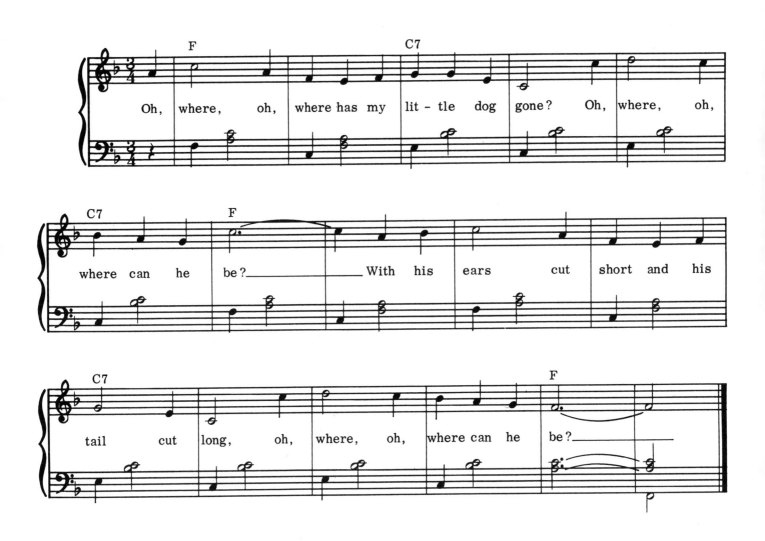

Oh, where, oh, where has my lit-tle dog gone? Oh, where, oh,

where can he be?_____ With his ears cut short and his

tail cut long, oh, where, oh, where can he be?_____

Wee Willie Winkie

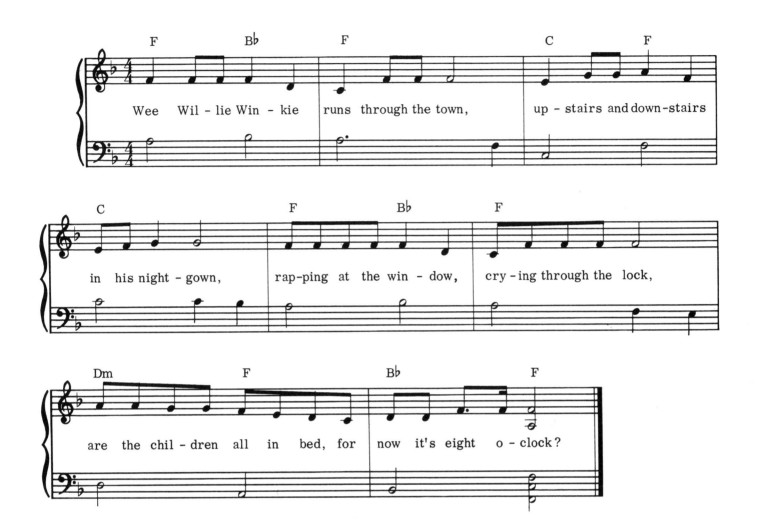

Wee Wil - lie Win - kie runs through the town, up - stairs and down-stairs in his night - gown, rap-ping at the win - dow, cry - ing through the lock, are the chil - dren all in bed, for now it's eight o - clock?

THREE WISE MEN OF GOTHAM

Three wise men of Gotham
Went to sea in a bowl;
If the bowl had been stronger,
My story would have been longer.

Yankee Doodle

Yan-kee Doo-dle went to town, a – rid-ing on a po – ny, he stuck a feath – er in his cap and called it mac-a-ron – i. Yan – kee Doo-dle doo-dle do, Yan-kee Doo-dle dan – dy, all the lass-ies are so smart and sweet as sug-ar can-dy.

THE QUEEN OF HEARTS

The Queen of Hearts she made some tarts,
All on a summer's day;
The Knave of Hearts he stole those tarts,
And took them clean away.

JACK SPRAT

Jack Sprat could eat no fat,
His wife could eat no lean,
And so between them both, you see,
They licked the platter clean.

COBBLER, COBBLER

Cobbler, cobbler, mend my shoe,
Get it done by half past two;
Stitch it up, and stitch it down,
Then I'll give you half a crown.

CLAP HANDS, CLAP HANDS

Clap hands, clap hands,
Till father comes home;
For father's got money,
But mother's got none.

Away in a Manger

CHRISTMAS IS COMING

Christmas is coming, the geese are getting fat,
Please to put a penny in the old man's hat.
If you haven't got a penny, a ha'penny will do;
If you haven't got a ha'penny, then God bless you!

Christ is Born in Bethlehem

E. CASWALL
J. GOSS

See a-mid the win - ter snow, born for us on earth be-low,

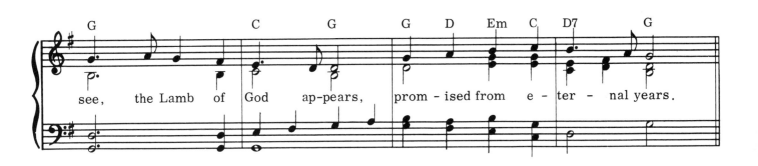

see, the Lamb of God ap-pears, prom - ised from e - ter - nal years.

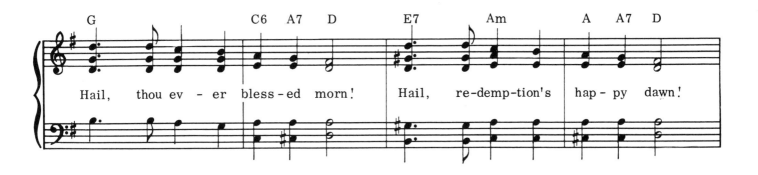

Hail, thou ev - er bless-ed morn! Hail, re-demp-tion's hap - py dawn!

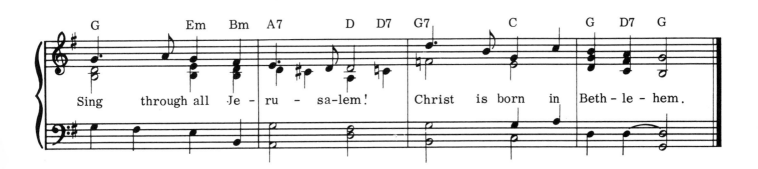

Sing through all Je - ru - sa-lem! Christ is born in Beth - le - hem.

Jesus Loves Me

ANNA B. WARNER

I Saw Three Ships

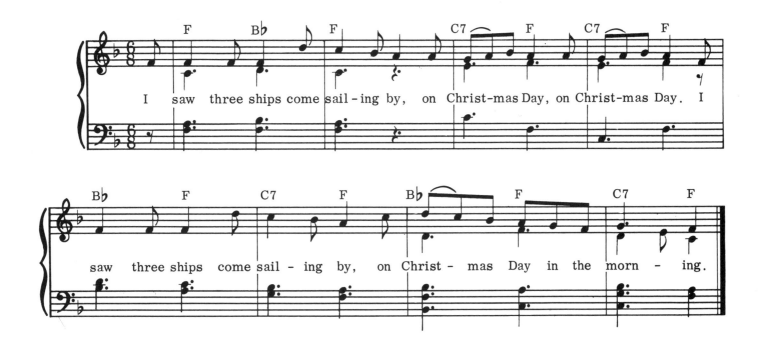

I saw three ships come sail-ing by, on Christ-mas Day, on Christ-mas Day. I saw three ships come sail-ing by, on Christ - mas Day in the morn - ing.

HOT CROSS BUNS

Hot cross buns! Hot cross buns!
One a penny, two a penny,
Hot cross buns!
If your daughters do not like them
Give them to your sons;
And if you have not any of these pretty little elves,
You cannot do better than eat them yourselves.

56

Jingle Bells

sleigh._____ Jin - gle bells, jin - gle bells, jin-gle all the way. Oh what fun it

is to ride in a one horse o - pen sleigh.

STAR LIGHT, STAR BRIGHT

Star light, star bright,
First star I see tonight,
I wish I may, I wish I might,
Have the wish I wish tonight.

Now I Lay Me Down to Sleep

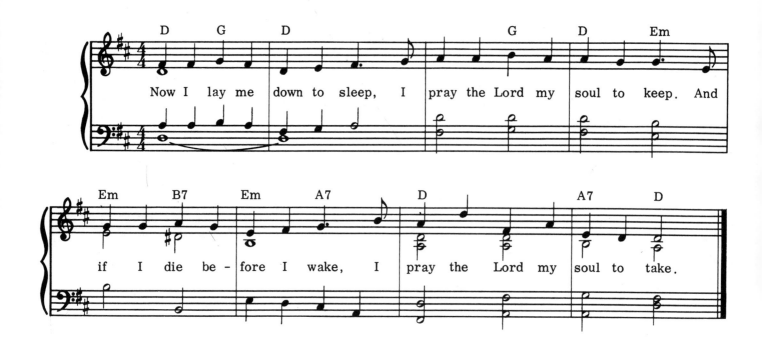

MATTHEW, MARK, LUKE, AND JOHN

Matthew, Mark, Luke, and John,
Bless the bed that I lie on.
Four corners to my bed,
Four angels round my head;
One to watch and one to pray
And two to bear my soul away.

EARLY TO BED

Early to bed,
And early to rise,
Makes a man healthy,
Wealthy, and wise.

Oh, Christmas Tree

Oh, Christ-mas Tree, oh, Christ-mas Tree, how ev-er-green your branch-es!

You nev-er change the whole year round, you bright-en up the snow-y ground. Oh,

Christ-mas Tree, oh, Christ-mas Tree, how ev-er-green your branch-es!

CHRISTMAS COMES BUT ONCE A YEAR

Christmas comes but once a year,
And when it comes it brings good cheer,
A pocket full of money, and a cellar full of beer.

'Twas the Night Before Christmas

CLEMENT CLARK MOORE
GORDON CLARKE

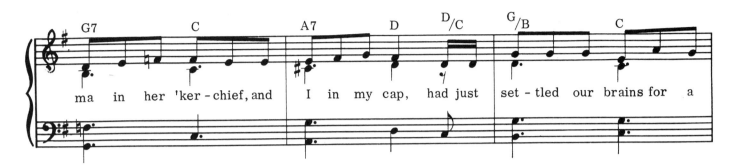

ma in her 'ker-chief, and I in my cap, had just set-tled our brains for a

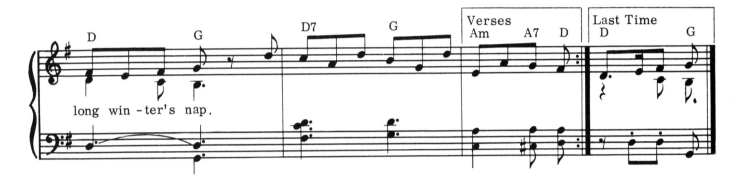

long win-ter's nap.

Extra verses

When out on the lawn there arose such a clatter,
I sprang from my bed to see what was the matter.
Away to the window I flew like a flash,
Tore open the shutters and threw up the sash.
The moon on the breast of the new-fallen snow,
Gave a lustre of midday to objects below,
When, what to my wondering eyes should appear,
But a miniature sleigh, and eight tiny reindeer;

With a little old driver, so lively and quick,
I knew in a moment it must be St. Nick.
More rapid than eagles his coursers they came,
And he whistled, and shouted, and called them by name;
"Now, Dasher! now, Dancer! now, Prancer and Vixen!
On, Comet! on, Cupid! on Donner and Blitzen!
To the top of the porch, to the top of the wall!
Now, dash away, dash away, dash away all!"

As dry leaves that before the wild hurricane fly,
When they meet with an obstacle, mount to the sky
So up to the house-top the coursers they flew,
With the sleigh full of toys, and St. Nicholas, too.
And then in a twinkling, I heard on the roof
The prancing and pawing of each little hoof.
As I drew in my head, and was turning around,
Down the chimney St. Nicholas came with a bound.

He was dressed all in fur from his head to his foot,
And his clothes were all tarnished with ashes and soot,
A bundle of toys he had flung on his back,
And he looked like a peddler just opening his pack.
His eyes how they twinkled! his dimples how merry!
His cheeks were like roses, his nose like a cherry,
His droll little mouth was drawn up like a bow,
And the beard of his chin was as white as the snow.

The stump of a pipe he held tight in his teeth,
And the smoke, it encircled his head like a wreath.
He had a broad face and a round little belly
That shook when he laughed, like a bowl full of jelly.
He was chubby and plump, a right jolly old elf,
And I laughed when I saw him, in spite of myself.
A wink of his eye, and a twist of his head,
Soon gave me to know I had nothing to dread.

He spoke not a word, but went straight to his work,
And filled all the stockings; then turned with a jerk,
And laying his finger aside of his nose,
And giving a nod, up the chimney he rose.
He sprang to his sleigh, to his team gave a whistle,
And away they all flew like the down of a thistle;
But I heard him exclaim, ere he drove out of sight,
"Happy Christmas to all, and to all a Good-night!"

THE HOUSE THAT JACK BUILT

This is the house
That Jack built.

This is the malt
That lay in the house
That Jack built.

This is the rat,
That ate the malt
That lay in the house
That Jack built.

This is the cat,
That killed the rat,
That ate the malt
That lay in the house
That Jack built.

This is the dog,
That worried the cat,
That killed the rat,
That ate the malt
That lay in the house
That Jack built.

This is the cow with the crumpled horn,
That tossed the dog,
That worried the cat,
That killed the rat,
That ate the malt
That lay in the house
That Jack built.

This is the maiden all forlorn,
That milked the cow with the crumpled horn,
That tossed the dog,
etc.

This is the man all tattered and torn,
That kissed the maiden all forlorn,
That milked the cow with the crumpled horn,
That tossed the dog,
etc.

This is the priest all shaven and shorn,
That married the man all tattered and torn,
That kissed the maiden all forlorn,
That milked the cow with the crumpled horn,
That tossed the dog,
etc.

This is the cock that crowed in the morn,
That waked the priest all shaven and shorn,
That married the man all tattered and torn,
That kissed the maiden all forlorn,
That milked the cow with the crumpled horn,
That tossed the dog,
etc.

This is the farmer sowing his corn,
That kept the cock that crowed in the morn,
That waked the priest all shaven and shorn,
That married the man all tattered and torn,
That kissed the maiden all forlorn,
That milked the cow with the crumpled horn,
That tossed the dog,
etc.

This is the horse and the hound and the horn,
That belonged to the farmer sowing his corn,
That kept the cock that crowed in the morn,
That waked the priest all shaven and shorn,
That married the man all tattered and torn,
That kissed the maiden all forlorn,
That milked the cow with the crumpled horn,
That tossed the dog,
etc.

THIRTY DAYS HATH SEPTEMBER

Thirty days hath September,
April, June, and November;
All the rest have thirty-one,
Excepting February alone,
And that has twenty-eight days clear
And twenty-nine in each leap year.

ONE, TWO, BUCKLE MY SHOE

1, 2,
Buckle my shoe;

3, 4,
Knock at the door;

5, 6,
Pick up sticks;

7, 8,
Lay them straight;

9, 10,
A big fat hen;

11, 12,
Dig and delve;

13, 14,
Maids a-courting;

15, 16,
Maids in the kitchen;

17, 18,
Maids in waiting;

19, 20,
My plate's empty.

Printed by Printwise (Haverhill) Limited, Suffolk 2/11 (177360)